Self Love vs Digital Lust

Written By: Dwayne Bryant, Ph.D..

First Edition
Publisher: Bryant Consulting Company
Oak City, North Carolina
ISBN: 9798599466307

All rights reserved No parts of this book may be reproduced, stored in retrieval systems, or transmitted in any form, by any means including mechanical, electronic, photocopying, recording or otherwise without prior permission of the publisher.

Introduction

Have you ever looked in the mirror, and all you see are imperfections? In a world of angles and filters, it's hard to see the true value in natural beauty. Instead of embracing your reflection, many are focused on the bulge at their waist, the stretch marks on their butt, and/or the blemishes on their skin. For some, it goes beyond looking in the mirror, as they wish they could do public speaking without stuttering, they wish that they were able to afford the designer clothing, jewelry, and cars you see on social media. The images we fill our minds with have an impact on how we view the quality of our lives. Too often we develop an emotional response to the images that prevent us from fully appreciating the natural gifts that we have.

The reality is that these images tell us that we are not enough. The idea of materialism is forced on us as children through music, holidays, and the media. In a perfect world, we would have someone to tell us that we are unique, and we are beautiful, strong, and enough. Love yourself or nobody will. There are many articles that discuss self-love and many try to practice the things they read. Yet, the applications of things are vastly different than the proposed theory. Regardless of how many times we promise ourselves that this time I will ferociously love on "me", the application is a whole lot harder, especially in the era of social media.

The journey of self-love is most difficult, but it is not impossible. In the same way, you can obsess about your imperfections and you can program your mind to obsess about your perfections. You have one life, one body, one mind, and one chance to truly love yourself. You can change the things you do not like; you can work on having a healthier lifestyle, mindset, and spirit. These things can be changed; however, you cannot leave your body and get another (unless you have surgery of course), so you may as well do yourself a favor and love the one you are in. The beauty in self-love is that you develop a healthier mind, and as a result, you live a healthier lifestyle. The journey to self-discovery can be a scary one because you come head-on with every part of yourself. You have to be blatantly honest with yourself about who you are. There will be areas you hate to look at, and it will SUCK!! However, once you get past the not-so-fun stuff, you can finally start defining yourself by your standards, and it can be a magical journey. Just remember that "the greatest of all these is love".

Chapter One
What is self-love?

Self-love is a natural and joyful connection with your body, mind, soul, and spirit. How you see yourself and what you think of yourself make up the perception and love you have for yourself. Loving yourself, accepting yourself, valuing yourself shows that you have high self-esteem. Acceptance, respect, and dignity make others appreciate you in the same way. Self-love depends exclusively on you, and, as a consequence, only you can love and appreciate the things that people can not physically see. Self-love reflects the relationship, feelings, and thoughts you have about your physical body, character, attitudes, and values. All of this will be reflected in how others see you and in your life in general.

Some characteristics of self-love are:

- Self Respect

- High Self-esteem,

- Solid Identity

- You feel happy and abundant

- You have a nice relationship with your physical body,

- You feel worthy to love and to be loved,

- You have confidence in yourself

- You do your best.

- You feel compassion for yourself.

- You are focused

Self-love reflects the relationship, feelings, and thoughts you have about your physical body, character, attitudes, and values. All this will be reflected in how others see you and in your life in general. If a person thinks about others and cares about them, then their self-love is in no way connected to egoism; it is easy and natural for them to love those around them.

In some instances, we misinterpret those who have a high value of self to be self-centered or arrogant. It surprises me that many people are offended by another person's ability to have confidence, assurance and self-love. The relationship that these individuals have with themselves speak volumes. A person of high value knows how to speak to themselves. Positive self-talk is a key element in knowing how to feed your mind in times of uncertainty. Knowing when to remove oneself from environments and conversations that don't serve them is comparable to aspects of relationship dynamics with others. In most cases we pay too much attention to what others think and have to say about us to truly focus on and do what's best for ourselves. Self-loving individuals naturally do not devote too much time to this, just like a good gardener does not require too much trouble in a well-kept garden. It is not difficult for a healthy and vigorous person to take care of themselves. Those who are concerned about self-love become, at least at first, more selfish - simply because the focus, in this case, begins to be on the self. Supplementing self-love with attention and care for others may not be difficult, but this is a completely separate work area.

When there is warmth in the soul, when there is light and sun in the soul, you feel the love, you have energy in your mind and body. You live with love. Sometimes, it is cold in your soul, and when you feel cold in your soul, you have no love. Sometimes it is dark in the inner world, and when the inner light goes out, love goes out. If you run out of strength to live, energy has gone - along with this.

Maintain the Light

Self-love is often thought to satisfy your simplest needs with pleasure, forgetting about responsibilities and other people. Allow yourself to do what you want, allow yourself to go shopping, surround yourself with romance, and make yourself presents. It is possible, but this love's level is the same as the love of a mother, whose child feeds mainly on lollipops and Coca-Cola, spending time mainly on computer games and other entertainment. Strictly speaking, it is difficult to call it a need. These are desires and whims that spoiled children insist on. The most important thing is that they do not provide joy for long, only while it is new and while others envy it. After a while, everything becomes boring; the joy goes away.

For example, sometimes people attempt to give themselves things like sleep, alcohol, food, shopping sprees while inside, everything is dreary. The world is gray, and the yearning for fulfillment is fed with useless acts and toxic liquids. It happens when a person is fond of shopping just because they feel bad about themselves. The satisfaction of needs in itself is not self-love, and it does not always end with inner joy, light, and warmth. You can't seriously fill yourself with any purchases. This is just some snag. A temporary measure, as a substitute for self-love - this is possible, but you should not believe the TV; this is not the joy of life, and this is not self-love. This is a poor-quality life.

Some begin to love themselves, while others do not. Satisfying one's needs is sometimes a substitute for self-love when a person seems to buy gifts because they don't love themselves. Of course, everyone's needs are different. If you need to move forward, grow, take care of other people, or the need to master any business with dignity you will have more reason to love yourself. You will have something to be proud of. If all the needs come down to food and entertain yourself with shopping or TV, then such self-love will hardly last.

Often, the following recipes are recommended as help and tips for "How to love yourself": "Accept yourself," "Do not gnaw yourself," "Forgive yourself and others," "Do not envy," "Be here and now." These are good guidelines. They do not just address self-love directly but how not to beat and torture yourself. If your boss has stopped swearing at you, does it mean that they now love you? If you have forgiven someone, it does not mean that that person has even become your friend. If you have risen from minus to zero about yourself, you have not yet risen to plus. This has nothing to do with the state of love, as a traumatologist has nothing to do with a cosmetologist's work. A traumatologist treats an injury; a beautician brings beauty to a healthy body. If a person comes with a sick soul, he needs to make repairs to their soul, but a soul without pain is not the same as a soul with love. These recommendations are not about love but repairs.

On the other hand, if the soul hurts, then first, you need to heal it. If it is completely dark in your soul, if there is a problematic swamp in your soul, then you cannot build a palace on such a swamp. Yes, you need to remove the victim's position, deal with the internal saboteur, remove limiting beliefs and bodily negativity, give up sweet idealizations, wean yourself off bad habits. There is a lot of work. Someone here will be shown treatment and psychotherapy, someone - the path of study, characteristic of the synthon approach... It is important to understand that you will not automatically love yourself when you have done all this difficult but crucial work. The house is renovated but not yet a holiday space. The holiday needs to be arranged separately. A repaired soul works flawlessly, and filling it with love is another, separate job.

Chapter Two
Social Media Use and Self-Love

In recent years social media has experienced widespread popularity within our society, starting from small personal web pages to full--blown mass communication networks where users can give or find almost any information about themselves or others within minutes. These sites have only been used by the computer--savvy to be incredibly user-friendly and spread worldwide. While the popularity of social networking sites continues to grow, so does the user's time on the page, even to the point of having the sites available on their mobile phone to check while away from the computer. As the number of time users spend on social networking sites continues to grow, their interactions with others offline tends to decrease, meaning that most of their socializing and socialization occur within the glow of a computer or phone screen.

One potential consequence of the individual's increased online interaction time is that the formation of identity and understanding of self is now affected, to a greater degree, through the popularity or feedback on certain aspects of the user's life that they are willing to share.

Social networking sites allow users to create electronic profiles for themselves, provide details about their life and experiences, post pictures, maintain relationships, plan social events, meet new people, comment on others' lives, express beliefs, preferences, and emotions fulfill belongingness needs.

Social networking sites can also serve as a basis for social comparisons, self-evaluation, or self-enhancement. Humans possess a fundamental drive to compare themselves with others. This serves many different functions such as fulfilling affiliation needs, evaluating the self, making decisions, inspiring and regulating emotions and well-being.

Upward social comparison occurs when comparing oneself to superior others with positive characteristics, while downward social comparison means comparing oneself with inferior others with negative characteristics. Although upward social comparison can be beneficial when it inspires people to become more like the person they look up to, it often causes people to feel inadequate, has poorer self-evaluations, and negatively affects them.

On the other hand, downward social comparison can make people feel negative (it shows how things could worsen). However, it often leads to improvement in effect and self-evaluation.

Recent studies have found that frequent Facebook users believe that other users are happier and more successful, especially when they do not know them very well offline. People compare their real offline selves to others' idealized online selves, which can be detrimental to well-being and self-evaluation.

Moreover, social networking sites also offer distinct information not available in offline settings such as information about the person's social network (number of people in the network, amount of engagement a person has with network members person with an active social network (receiving many comments and likes) is usually perceived as an upward comparison target in terms of popularity, sociability, and perceived social capital.

As a result of chronic or occasional exposure to upward comparisons on social media sites, there could be a negative impact on people's self-evaluation and self-esteem. Every day, chronic social media use may affect trait self-esteem negatively, while state self-esteem can also be affected by incidental use. Research shows that people who use Facebook frequently report higher depression rates and decreased well-being.

Some Popular Social Networks

Social networks in recent years are changing rapidly. This evolution speed is enhanced for young people, who are often more willing to try new applications. It is combined with a real diversity of practices that vary according to age, social background, geographic area, and local habits and fashions. Thus, the exact knowledge of existing networks will inevitably have their limits. There is no doubt that a few months after the publication of these lines, new tools will be used or that the old ones' use will have changed. It is mainly a question of trying to understand the general functionalities and take some height in these phenomena.

Some of the most used social networks are:

1. Facebook

No need to present Facebook or its functionalities. With over 25 billion users globally, the network remains undoubtedly the most common social network. The tool is widely used for all ages. Messenger remains widely used, and the company Facebook also owns two of the tools listed below, which are particularly popular with adolescents: WhatsApp and Instagram. Thanks to this trio, the company has a significant place in young people's digital social life.

2. WhatsApp

WhatsApp is an application for a smartphone. It offers an instant messaging service via the Internet. It is not necessarily used as a social networking service. However, it offers the possibility of creating "discussion groups," quickly allowing a group of users to discuss. Group messaging can strengthen affinity groups and can play a role in social relationships. Other applications are sometimes used for the same use of chat and discussion groups (Telegram, Viber, Facebook Messenger, Snapchat recently ...), the issues are the same.

3. Instagram

Instagram is a smartphone application. It offers a service for sharing photos and short videos. It is particularly known for his "filters," which will significantly modify photos and easily make them more attractive. Users will follow the accounts of interest to them, whether their friends, celebrities, or business communications. The publication of photos and videos is accompanied by short texts. Still, it remains focused on the visual, which appears to be very mastered by young people: the photos posted must participate in a good representation of their person. The tool does not directly allow you to share someone else's content, so the display will mainly show tracked accounts' outputs. Instagram is known to favor engagement from people who easily like photos.

4. YouTube

The video-sharing platform owned by Alphabet (the parent company of Google) is used by young people (and the not-so-young) to follow all the videos from videographers and content producers that appeal to them. However, for this, it includes many social network features, and it is common for young people to exchange videos there, but also, and above all, directly produce them. There are colossal amounts of videos of all kinds, with a few dozen views corresponding to groups of quite young friends or acquaintances of no real interest to those who do not belong to this circle.

5. Periscope

In the video category, it seems necessary to talk about Periscope and, more generally, applications allowing to transmit video live. The application allows you to film (and film yourself) and broadcast the video live. It includes various mechanisms specific to social networks: subscribing to be notified of live streams (or see recordings), chat function, "likes," etc. Developed by Twitter, the two services are closely linked. There are many young people filming themselves in front of the camera without doing anything very specific (playing the guitar, watching television, etc.) other than interacting with the chat. Still, others carry out telephone "hoaxes" or challenges live. The practices are much smaller in volume than other services, but the impacts can be substantial.

6. Twitter

Twitter is a leading social network by number of users. Its main function is to publish short messages of less than 140 characters. These messages are necessarily public, and "Twittos" (Twitter users) are invited to share them (ReTweet / like / reply). They can be embellished with photos or videos. The site also allows you to send private messages with no size limits as soon as users follow each other. The practices are very diverse on Twitter. Many middle school and high school students use it to comment on their daily lives and react to news that affects them. It's easier to interact with Twitter under a pseudonym than on Facebook. While no one imagines that tweets are private, the resharing features can message a much larger audience than initially imagined.

7. Snapchat

This application (on a smartphone) is very popular with young people. It allows the exchange of messages, photos, or short videos, which is that the lifespan of the messages is limited. Thus, upon receipt of the "Snap," it will only be displayed for a certain time (a few seconds for most messages, 24 hours in certain specific cases) before disappearing. The tone can be lighter there without fear that the words or photos will come out at other times. The service is fun-oriented and also makes it easy to edit photos, especially self-portraits ("selfies") with transformative filters (adding attributes, deformation or swapping of the face, etc.). This application poses real problems in terms of confidentiality. Indeed, its users expect that messages cannot be preserved while methods continue to allow their recording. Also, the company itself can access the content after it is erased from the phones.

This list is necessarily limited. Keep in mind that many interactions similar to those performed on social media can take place through online video games where identity issues are often less important. The phenomenon seems to have died out, but sites offering opportunities for anonymous questions such as

While social media can be a wonderful tool, offering access to information about a wide range of people and allowing unlimited networking opportunities, there is a potential downside to frequent social media use. As people use social media sites in their everyday life, they risk overexposure to upward social comparison information that can have a cumulative negative effect on their well-being.

Moreover, when people with low self-esteem use social media sites to express themselves in what seems like a safe environment, they could get into a vicious cycle of receiving some social support and being exposed to constant upward social comparison, which may impair their self-esteem further.

Chapter Three
Social Media's Impact on Self-Love

Social media has been linked to higher loneliness, envy, anxiety, depression, narcissism and decreased social skills. The narratives we share and portray on social media are all positive and celebratory. It's a hybridized digital version of "Keeping up with the Joneses." Meaning for some, sometimes it appears everyone you know is in significant relationships, taking 5-star vacations, and living your dream life. However, what is shared across our social networks only broadcasts the positive aspects of our lives-the highlight reels.

Since we're only getting people's highlight reels and comparing them to ourselves, it is natural to react to what we're watching. How do these impact relationships and our love life? Research shows that:

- 60% of people using social media reported that it impacted their self-love in a negative way

- 50% reported social media having negative effects on their relationships

- 80% reported that it is easier to be deceived by others through their sharing on social media

Paradox Effect

It seems that social media is creating a paradox effect: giving off the illusion of many choices while making it harder to find viable options. Can it be that our highly connected world has now become disconnected? Dr. Jennifer Rhodes, a licensed psychologist, relationship expert, and the founder of the bi-coastal relationship consultancy, Rapport Relationships, explains, "My clients that are a little obsessed with following dates on social media do lack the skills to communicate effectively in person. This lack of security and communication skills most definitely increases anxiety and depression. I see so much anxiety related to dating and how to navigate texting & communication that I have started to use Social Fitness training to teach assertiveness skills with my clients".

Posting dinners, selfies, and vacation photos over human interaction for some is interaction. That is their interaction. Natalia Lusinski, Sex, Dating, and Relationships writer for Bustle, says, "I feel couples forget how to talk in real life, with all the texting and social media-updating that they do. They seem to know everything about each other and each other's days already, so they don't feel the need to talk much in person."

The paradox effect in dating is creating the illusion of having more social engagement, social capital, and popularity but masking one's true persona. Since some are interfacing digitally more than physically, it is much easier to emotionally manipulate others because they are reliant on what I call "Vanity Validation." For some, the one you portray on your networks and the true you create a double consciousness. Your lauded self on social media is constantly seeking more validation through electronic likes, not life. I feel many people convey all the positive pics, updates, etc. — but then, once you date them, you realize there are several other layers to them, not just the positive façade they convey online. For some, projecting what they want people to see and getting likes, plusses, re-tweets, and shares helps them feel better about themselves and connected to others.

Self-Esteem and Vanity Validation

In the latest Match Singles in America study's findings on how social media has impacted people's dating lives, they found that 57% of singles say social media has generated a Fear Of Missing Out (FOMO). Dr. Suzana Flores, author of Facehooked: How Facebook Affects our Emotions, Relationships, and Lives, explains, "When someone interacts over social media for prolonged periods, inevitably they feel compelled to continue to check for updates. I call this the "Slot Machine Effect" in that when we receive a like or a comment to a post, or when we come across an interesting new post from someone else, we experience what psychologists refer to as intermittent reinforcement—sometimes we get rewarded with an exciting post. Sometimes we are not, but the rewards through external validation of our posts cause us to remain digitally connected.

The "Slot Machine Effect" and comparing ourselves to others is just one side of FOMO. Match reported 51% say social media has made them feel more self-conscious about their appearance. Research has also shown that Facebook users are becoming increasingly depressed from comparing themselves to their profile. Meaning that if a person's reality does not match the digital illusion they post on their profiles, emotionally, one may feel they are not living up to the best form of themselves.

Emotionally secure people do not struggle as much with these issues. However, a large portion of our population have emotional insecurities, and these folks are the ones that would benefit from a dating consultation to provide them with the tools and support to learn how to more effectively communicate their needs and desires. Social media and texting have made it all too easy to default to one's perception rather than remain curious about what may be going on.

This is just an aspect of what is occurring in today's rapidly evolving digital world. For us to accept these behaviors with disregard for how it impacts us emotionally is what the core of what I call, The Millennial Virus. What is it doing to our sense of self? Are we becoming more narcissistic? Are we becoming more insecure? Are technology driving dating, sex, and emotion? Are dating patterns just an extension of how we behave on social networks?

Self-Love vs. Digital Lust

Reflection on love in the age of dating apps and social networks of this world.

It is well known: our world moves fast. The lives of our electronic devices are shortened; we quickly get tired of our wardrobe. The same goes for human relationships, which seem to be building up as quickly as they are breaking down.

Our relationships are built in less than two like the toy of a Kinder Surprise. It's a real race against time. Watch out if you want to take your time to brush your fingertips into the heart of a potential love before you go into business. You have to be in a relationship and quickly.

The flame, subject to the slightest breath, goes out quickly. Few people still seek to wander into the darkest recesses of their suitor's mind. From now on, everyone is just looking to warm up in a hurry. We stay on the surface. The other half has become an individual as lonely as us, whose presence we tolerate only because it accompanies us to not be alone. Modern love is selfish. We are in the era of individualism, the dictatorship of hedonism. We want to enjoy everything here and now. We want to share the world with one person, set ablaze, light fireworks, then get bored and just, slowly... go away.

The vulnerability has become a real sin: we are afraid of words of love, the real ones, those who stain the tongue in pink and make flowers grow in the eyes' hollow. We are afraid to get naked, I mean really: by keeping all our clothes but leaving to see what we have more personal, more intimate.

The greatness of feeling has been replaced by something mundane, superficial. Now, we share a little piece of his life with a person who accidentally packed our photo on the right. The time is disillusioned: carnal desire replaces the butterflies in the belly, which flee the minute we glimpse the demons that inhabit his/her partner.

Our society's hunger for excessive gluttony also applies to bodies, which have become consumer goods like any other, with an expiry date. Like what it is, not only the objects whose obsolescence is programmed.

Loyalty has become a supreme value in this age where no one belongs to no one. Jealousy is synonymous with affection.

Despite these networks that allow us to connect anywhere at any time of the day, loneliness is omnipresent. So when you meet someone, you become addicted: more able to wake up without a text from that person, more able to do great things on your own, as a full human, without that person either by our side.

In short, it's a crazy time to love someone. Despite everything, I wish you to meet someone who makes you trip, knees shaky and eyes shining, yes, if it still exists. Wish you find someone, not because you liked their profile picture, but because your minds are laughing at the same jokes that no one understands or because when you are chatting, the world suddenly seems to make more sense. I wish you someone who will take pleasure in understanding why you always cry at the end of this particular film, why you bite your nails when we talk about the future or why you have the mania to pick up all the beautiful pebbles that cross your route.

The influence of social networks on our self-love

Today, we are constantly sharing moments of our life on the Internet. We display our photos, videos, and thoughts in the hope of receiving a "Like" in return. Why? Do we need the approval of people we don't often see to feel that our life is exciting?

The reality is that this can mean a high influence of social media on our self-esteem. And not just because of the number of interactions we get with a post. Although we are not fully aware of it, there are more factors to consider to avoid using new technologies to avoid self-esteem issues.

"You were once what you had. Today you are what you share." -**Godfried Bogaard**

The Impact of social media posts in our self-esteem

It is common to follow the social networks of influencers, brands, or magazines whose publications are closer to advertising than to people's daily lives in general. The purpose of these publications is to cover a specific product.

Unrealistic images of how we should be ourselves and our daily life are transmitted to our mobile phones. We are given a stereotype of beauty and lifestyle that is difficult to achieve. This can cause discomfort. This is part of the impact of social media on our self-esteem.

The conflict Internal appears when we see that our reality does not match what it is supposed to be. These publications can lead us to set unrealistic and difficult to achieve goals. So our self-esteem goes down when we find that we won't.

The pace of life that others follow in social media is difficult for ordinary people to achieve. We can't afford to travel as much as they can. Nor to eat in the same places and live in the same houses. But that doesn't mean our life is worse. Our life is just different.

The impact of social media on our self-esteem is seen in our self-image

The reality is that it doesn't just affect the goals we can set for ourselves in life. The major impact is not even at this level. The major problem of social networks on our self-esteem is linked to each person's self-image. The point is, the self-image that everyone wants for themselves is often quite close to the prototype reflected by influencers and brands on social media. The impact of all this on self-esteem is all the greater as the exposure time increases, as does the frequency of connection to social networks. As you can imagine, the greatest risk is that eating disorders develop.

This situation does not only affect women. A study found that men also sought to resemble men with muscular bodies that appear in the media. The difference between the two sexes is that men are less concerned with reaching the canon of beauty.

"A human is behind every tweet, blog, and email. Remember that." **Chris Brogan**

We also cannot forget that this does not happen to everyone. Having good self-esteem is a protective factor against everything we've been talking about. Therefore, it is crucial to realize the importance of other aspects of life to feel good about preserving our psychological well-being ... For a real impact of social networks on our self-esteem!

In recent years, the concept of human relations has grown enormously and become more complex, mainly because of the advent of social networks. These websites change our perception of others and the relationships we have with them for better or for worse.

Social Media and Self-Doubt

How can you resist the pressure created by artfully curated social media feeds? Magazines and advertising have long been criticized for upholding dangerously unrealistic standards of success and beauty, but at least it's acknowledged that they are idealized. These days, however, the impossible standards are set much closer to home, not by celebrities and models but by classmates and friends. With social media, teens can curate their lives. The resulting feeds read like highlight reels, showing only the best and most desirable moments while concealing efforts, struggles, and the merely ordinary aspects of day-to-day life. And there's evidence that those images are causing distress for many people.

Donna Wick, founder of Mind-to-Mind Parenting, says that for teenagers, the combined weight of vulnerability, the need for validation, and a desire to compare themselves with peers' forms what she describes as a "perfect storm of self-doubt." She's so thin. Her grades are perfect. Her body shape. What a happy couple. I'll never be that cool, that skinny, that lucky, and that successful. Sometimes, looking at friends' feeds "makes you feel like everyone has it together, but, you."

Struggling to stay afloat

The fallout from these unrealistic standards becomes more dangerous once young people reach college, where they face higher stakes, harder work, and a largely parent-free environment. The pressure to look perfect for impressing new peers, not to speak of friends and family back home, can be even greater.

After a recent spate of college suicides, researchers at Stanford University coined the phrase "duck syndrome." The term refers to how a duck appears to glide effortlessly across a pond while below the surface, its feet work frantically, invisibly struggling to stay afloat.

Several students who have died had projected a perfect image on social media—their feeds packed with inspirational quotes and filtered images showing attractive, happy people who seemed to excel with minimal effort. But behind the digital curtain, they were struggling emotionally.

Hiding imperfection

For people experiencing anxiety or depression, carefully edited feeds can act as a smokescreen, masking serious issues behind pretend perfection and making it harder for people or friends to see that they need help.

"It's important to remember that just posting edited pictures online or pretending your life is a little more glamorous than it is non itself a problem. Social media alone is unlikely to be at the heart of the issue, but it can make a difficult situation even harder.

People who have created idealized online personas may feel frustrated and depressed at the gap between who they pretend to be online and who they truly are. Another more prevalent problem is that their social feeds can become fuel for negative feelings they have about themselves for some people. People struggling with self-doubt read into their friends' images what they feel they are lacking.

People view social media through the lens of their own lives. If they're struggling to stay on top of things or suffering from low self-esteem, they're more likely to interpret images of peers having fun as confirmation that they're doing badly compared to their friends.

Social media and teenagers: How to help

What can parents do to help kids build a safe and reasonable relationship with social media before they're out on their own?

Keeping teens from falling into the social media trap is more complicated than it sounds. It's not about taking the phone away or having a single conversation. Parents need to be diligent about making sure kids are getting a dose of reality and modeling healthy behaviors.

- Take social media seriously. Don't underestimate the role social media plays in the lives of teenagers. "The power of a visual image is so strong. It's disorienting." Many teens never knew a world where social media didn't exist, and for them, the things that happen online—slights, break-ups, likes, or negative comments—are very real. When you talk about social media, make sure you're listening and be careful not to dismiss or minimize your teen's experiences.

• Encourage them to think outside the (crop) box. When you talk to your child about social media, encourage her to explore it more critically. A great way to start is to try asking her what she thinks has been cropped or edited out of her friends' "perfect" pictures and why. That can lead to larger questions. Do you think your friends are the people they appear to be online? Are you? What's the purpose of posting a photo? What is it about getting "likes" that feel good? Does looking at social media affect your mood?

• Model a healthy response to failure. Kids have to get the message that it is okay to fail, not only that it's okay to fail, but that is showing it is okay, too. If parents hide their failures, kids are less likely to be okay with anything less than success.

When things don't work out as you'd planned or a project goes awry, show your child how to accept it with grace. Let kids know that failure is part of how we learn to succeed, that it's nothing to be ashamed of, and let them see you pick yourself up and try again.

- Praise (and show) effort. The effort is something to be proud of. It can't be said enough.

Parents should let kids know that showing their work is something to be praised, not hidden. When your child has worked hard on something, praise her efforts no matter what the outcome. It's also helpful to examine how comfortable you are showing your efforts, especially those that don't succeed. Being proud and open about your work sets a powerful example for your child.

- Go on a "social holiday." If you're worried that your child is getting too wrapped up in social media, try taking a social holiday. If you're asking your child to take a break, practice what you preach and pledge to stay off media as well. It can be every bit as hard for parents to unplug as kids.

- Trust people, not pictures. Finally, don't rely on social media to let you know how your child is doing. She may post smiling selfies all day long, but if she seems unhappy or sounds unhappy on the phone, don't let it go. Ensure she knows it's safe to talk to you by encouraging her to share her feelings and supporting her when she does. Reassure her that you're not disappointed, and let her know you're proud of her for reaching out. "I'm so glad you called. It sounds like you're feeling overwhelmed, I'm here, and I love you. Let's talk this through together."

In the end, as a parent, you want your child to be happy and successful. But making sure she knows you love her and you're proud of her as she is—unfiltered, unedited, and imperfect—will help her build the confidence she needs to accept herself and stay safe and healthy when she's out on her own.

Chapter Four

What Selfies Are Doing to Self-Esteem in The Social Media Era

How they can exacerbate insecurity, anxiety, and depression? In case you've ever wondered how much time your daughter spends taking selfies, a poll in 2015 found that the average woman between 16 and 25 years old spends over five hours a week. It sounds like a lot unless you've tried to take selfies yourself and know what an elaborate process it can be. According to the poll, women average seven shots to get one image. Then there are the filters, not to mention real-life alterations like changing lighting or touching up makeup. You can also use apps for more drastic procedures like changing your bone structure, slimming your waistline, erasing pimples, and more. Of course, selfies can be silly and lighthearted. But there is a problem when photos become a measure of self-worth. With makeup, with retouch, with filters, multiple attempts, it's almost like you're never going to stack up. And that is where it begins to get dangerous.

We're used to worrying about how girls will be affected by seeing too many air-brushed images of models in magazines or movies. But now young people themselves are the models, and they're wielding their image-editing software. This leads to a lot of self-scrutiny as they try to perfect their images and compare their peers' pictures. Experts are understandably worried about what this means for kids' self-esteem.

Seeking Perfection

If you've been telling your daughter that she's beautiful just the way she is, she's getting a different message when she opens up Snapchat and sees filters and lenses that alter appearances. Pictures used to be final; now we have post-production.

Some of the filters are fun and distort in amusing ways, but also, there's a so-called "pretty filter" on Instagram and Snapchat. Beautifying filters are used almost reflexively by many, which means girls are getting used to seeing their peers effectively airbrushed every day online. There are also image altering apps that teens can download for more substantial changes. Facetune is one popular one, but there are many, and they can be used to do everything from erasing pimples to change your face's structure or make you look taller. One app called RetouchMe gives your photo a "professional retouch" using a photo editing team for under a dollar.

The possibilities can be overwhelming, particularly since girls know they are scrutinized on their appearance — as, of course, they are scrutinizing their peers.

Too much comparison

Self-Love vs. Digital Lust

Self-love often takes a hit when you start comparing yourself too much to other people, which social media seems to be made for. One study found that frequently viewing selfies led to decreased self-esteem and decreased life satisfaction. Another study found that girls who spend more time looking at pictures on Facebook reported higher weight dissatisfaction and self-objectification.

In her book *Enough As She Is*, Rachel Simmons writes about pressures facing girls, including comparing themselves to peers on social media and feeling that they were coming up short. One 18-year-old girl told her, "I don't hate myself when I'm alone. I just hate myself in comparison to other people."

Thanks to social media, that time alone in your head that most adults grew up with has been eroded. Any spare moment she has, a young woman now might easily open up Instagram or Snapchat, which means that she starts playing the comparison game.

Even if the pictures a girl posts on social media get plenty of likes, she might still feel insecure — especially if she's an adolescent who is already feeling insecure and trying to make herself feel better. That's because humans tend to be very "mood consistent." It can feel icky to do something on the outside that is inconsistent with how we feel inside. That's why if you're feeling sad, you might be more likely to want to listen to sad music instead of watching a comedy. Similarly, if you are judgmental and negative about yourself, it generally takes more than a good selfie to pull yourself out of that trap.

Mental Health Consequences

While social media might not cause a mental health disorder, it can pull some kids closer into a diagnosable range if they are already struggling. If you're depressed or anxious, you're probably going to be comparing yourself to others more, or devaluing yourself more. Maybe you'll be striving even harder to try and 'catch up,' which is an impossible feat.

The problem of selfies has even attracted various professional journals for plastic surgeons, which have been posting articles about increasing requests for plastic surgery coming from young people. A poll from the American Academy of Facial Plastic and Reconstructive Surgeons found that 42% of surgeons were asked to perform procedures for improved selfies and pictures on social media platforms. The journal Plastic and Reconstructive Surgery published an article called "When Is Teenage Plastic Surgery Versus Cosmetic Surgery Okay?" exploring the safety and ethical considerations of performing different procedures and providing "cosmetic medication" Botox and fillers to adolescent clients.

There is even a term for kids who are fixating on their appearance because of social media —

selfie dysmorphia, which is imes called Snapchat dysmorphia. While this isn't a real diagnosis, it is a term that recognizes that more people are experiencing dysmorphia or the idea that there is something fundamentally flawed in their appearance.

It also gestures to a diagnosis that is real: body dysmorphic disorder, which is a mental health disorder related to OCD. People with body dysmorphic disorder are obsessed with what they perceive to be a disfiguring flaw, like a large nose or ears, a blemish on the skin, or underdeveloped muscles. These flaws might be imagined or very minor and blown out of proportion.

While most children won't develop body dysmorphic disorder or even so-called selfie dysmorphia, they can still exist somewhere on the spectrum of fixating on their appearance, just as they might struggle with anxiety depression, whether or not they are at a clinical level.

Building Self-Esteem

Prioritizing our appearance is nothing new in society, but with selfies, children get inundated with the feedback that how they look is important. That's why it is up to parents to make sure their children are getting the message that what they think and do is even more important. Don't hold back from complimenting your children on their appearance, but make an effort to compliment them at least as much for the things they do and how hard they work.

While it is good for anyone's self-esteem to like the way they look, it is crucial to have many self-esteem sources.

Having a personal interest in something and seeing how your skills grow with time and effort makes you feel proud of what you can do and focuses away from achieving perfection, which is impossible. It also encourages children to look inside themselves for their self-esteem (and not just to compliments from others), which is an important part of growing into a happy, confident woman.

How to develop self-love in the social media era

Something I love about social media is that it allows me to keep in touch with distant friends, learn about other ideas, or get inspired. But on the other hand, comparison, which is a normal impulse, can be harmful to your self-esteem.

When you view your social networks, you must be aware that what you see is the edited and improved version of what your contacts want to show.

You are comparing yourself to their carefully crafted photographs and phrases. It would seem that they have the perfect life but remember that they do not. As Seth Stephens says in his book

Self-Love vs. Digital Lust

Everybody Lies, people lie to Facebook, but they tell the truth to Google.

Beautiful photos of happy people on the beach can cause not only delight but also self-dislike. Looking at such photos, we often begin to criticize ourselves uncontrollably. And we no longer notice how the next time, taking our photo, we look at it with self-loathing, retouch flaws and scold our shortcomings. Remember that by loving ourselves, we can give this love to the world. So, everyone benefits from this! How to get rid of self-dislike in the era of social networks? Try these five ways.

1. When you are taking pictures, look at the whole picture.

How often do we take a picture and immediately zoom in to test ourselves? Think about group photos: What's the first thing people do when they look at him? They focus on themselves and their flaws. But it is our imperfections that make us who we are. When you take a photo, try to see the whole image - the whole scene. Think about where you were, who you were with, and how you felt. The photographs should capture memories, not project fantasies.

2. Uninstall picture editing applications from your phone. Eliminate the temptation!

Striving for excellence can border on obsession. Combining this with social media addiction is a recipe for disaster. Just as it is good to have no alcohol in the house when you are on addiction treatment, removing the apps will remove the temptation. Instead, fill your phone with apps to help you develop creatively. Try to learn a new language, play mind games, and listen to interesting podcasts. Take pictures of the larger dog. You probably don't want to change anything in it.

3. Unsubscribe from those who provoke your dislike for yourself.

Self-Love vs. Digital Lust

Watch yourself. If you don't stop comparing yourself to models while reading fashion magazines, give up magazines. Yes, we already know that photos are retouched in magazines, but now such images are looking at us from social networks. Since they appear on someone's channels and not in magazines, we often think of them as real. If you constantly feel bad looking at other people's posts, unsubscribe. Instead, find people who will inspire you by encouraging self-confidence.

Don't follow people who make you feel insecure, follow good friends and people who really inspire you. Another thing, your followers are not your friends.

Also, avoid making viewing your networks the first thing you do in the morning. Keep in mind that before going to sleep, watching social networks can affect you more, since you will be tired and your emotions will be more on the surface.

4. Get out of social networks and immerse yourself in the real world.

Behold. Put your phone aside. Observe reality: from 85-year-old walking with a 10-year-old grandson to a couple hugging on a park bench. Take a look around to see how diverse, unique, and interesting we are all. Life is Beautiful!

5. The next time you take a photo, find one thing in yourself that you love.

We will always find flaws! Shift your focus to dignity. The next time you take a photo, instead of looking for what to fix, look for what you like. If you can't find anything at the beginning, take a look at the photo as a whole. Great outfit? Beautiful place? Wonderful people in the photo? Start training your brain to see beauty. It can (and should) start in the mirror. Every day tell yourself that you love yourself, find one reason for what. The reason is not necessarily external. Remember, the more we learn to love ourselves, the more love we can give to others.

Chapter Five
Self-Love is a Job

The most amazing, most amazing answer is that conceptually it's simple. It's just not for everyone, but only for mentally healthy people. A person who is not in a mentally healthy space will have trouble finding peace and fully receiving love. How long does it take to love yourself? How long does it take to turn on the light in the apartment? A good host has one second to flip the switch. Suppose you come to visit friends, or want to wish a bright person a happy birthday ... Remember what is happening to you: right away, the very second you see the birthday boy, you charge yourself with joy, you charge yourself with light and warmth and convey to this good person everything you want to tell him. If your baby woke up at night and cried: you need to get up and also swing him, and even with love because otherwise, he will not fall asleep. What are you doing? You jump up at the same second and turn to him with love because it is necessary. Where do you get this love? Out of thin air, nowhere? This is just the ability to love, a common skill, and those who know how to include light and joy in their souls do it easily. It's no more difficult than feeding yourself and your kids three times a day something tasty (and healthy). If you are good at making breakfast, deal with that too. Start loving yourself, you will like it, and after that, you will do it for the rest of your life.

However, not everything is easy for us. We will always "do", even if it is in our interests. We have many different interests, and the game of boredom has its internal benefits. Lovely beautiful girls know how to flare up with joy at times, but just like that, will turn to sorrow. They do not want to warm themselves with light and warmth, they do not want to turn on energy until they pamper themselves in meeting their needs. The consumer society and all those accustomed to making money on women inspire women that a woman who loves herself can please herself with purchases. They suggest that shopping is an integral part of women's self-love. There have already been studies that have shown that shopping for modern women is a more therapeutic procedure than visiting a psychologist.

Women know how useful a massage is for health, how massage is a source of joy. All magazines write to women that massage is a miraculous procedure and that only these secret oriental techniques will return all your health. It's true; massage is really helpful. Men can learn a lot from the acts of self-care from women. However, massage therapists are not the same as psychologists. A massage therapist only needs to take part in the holiday that you create for yourself, just pat you in all the places you like, you will do the rest yourself. This is a form of maintenance that one needs to ensure that they are practicing a level of self-care that meets their needs. A massage is useful for health, but the beauty is that when a person is pleased, they are full of joy.

In total, be careful: self-love does not begin when you satisfy your needs, but after that, when you like yourself, and you decide to love yourself, that is, you turn on your light, warmth, and living energy within yourself. Accordingly, you can begin to love yourself immediately, without waiting for anything from yourself.

If you love yourself, you give yourself the power and right to rule your life. You will choose to become the author of your life. Start by never complaining. It's okay to ask for help, but it's not okay to complain. Complaining is experiencing your helplessness, which you have created. It's empty. If you love yourself, you will give up the offense: being offended is just a childish habit. We immerse ourselves in resentment, do ourselves badly so that they pay attention to us, and give us what we want.

When we are not given, we are offended again, but this no longer works because it worked in childhood, and in the adult world, you are doing yourself badly for nothing.

The one who loves knows and remembers their strengths and dignity well. Many people need to learn this too, and sometimes it's easier to start by noticing the virtues in the people around them. Take it into your work to write ten new merits of yourself and ten merits of someone from your loved ones, acquaintances, or work colleagues every day. When you know at any second that you are a worthy person living among worthy people, it will be easier to love yourself. If you love yourself, you will make your inner world light, and then the outer world, sanctified by the light of your soul, will become beautiful for you. If you love yourself very much, you will turn on the warmth in your soul, and you will become comfortable.

How to do this?

Make a list of what makes you happy, and cross out everything harmful from there. Choose the best for yourself, and after that, just do not be lazy to please yourself! As a background to life, master the exercise "Good, and you will feel good, and then you will consolidate your success with the exercise" Sunny." The sun is an expression of the inner. The sun is a must for the morning, begin it with a smile.

To have enough strength for this, start going to bed on time, that is, today, During the day, keep track of your rest, do not work drearily, and weariness: either give yourself a rest or work vigorously. This is done by all who love themselves.

If you love yourself, you will start to live in an organized way, start writing your tasks for the day and plan for the week, and later - and goals for the year. The one who loves himself makes sure that his life does not go stupidly, not accidentally, but in the

Self-Love vs. Digital Lust

direction that beckons you, in the direction where you see prospects.

If you love yourself, you will believe in yourself, and you will set big goals for your height. The one who loves himself shortsighted sets himself small goals to not strain now - and is forced to strain later, when he is no longer satisfied with what he has. Putting off going to the doctor, you only accumulate problems, and if you love yourself, you will go to the doctor, even if it is now troublesome and uncomfortable. It is not the one who loves himself who sits in a comfortable chair, but the one who lifts himself out of the trenches. If you love yourself, you will always learn. Imagine - you believing in yourself, believing in your future, you believe that this is the best you can pass on to your children. You have enough intelligence, culture, soul, light, love, sun and joy, so do it! This is the result of always learning. You will have the maximum of life and a plan for its implementation, and you will be proud of yourself, knowing that you deserve it! Then you have something to pass on to your children. You have something to give to the world and if you don't know-how, you have to learn.

Focus on your self-love

When was the last time you told yourself I love me? Or some positive word that made you feel proud of yourself? We spend half our lives wanting to please others, maintain a good reputation, be good at something for others, but very seldom do we stop to evaluate how we get along with ourselves. What types of beliefs we have about ourselves and what value we give ourselves in life. Stop and evaluate why you satisfy others' expectations so much and not your own. Why? If you had a relationship with yourself, what things would you do to make that relationship work? Therein lies the task. We seldom recognize that getting along with ourselves is like maintaining a relationship. For true love, my friend is how we love ourselves. We give what we are and have.

In psychological consultations, most of the cases treated have a lot to do with what we know as self-esteem. Self-esteem is a mixture of beliefs, thoughts, and evaluations that we have with ourselves. How we look at ourselves and how we accept ourselves. Talking about self-esteem is talking about a very fashionable topic and at the same time difficult to identify when we live it ourselves, since many times we believe that appreciating ourselves and showing affection to ourselves can lead us to narcissism.

Self-love is a day-to-day task and that task, everything in life, needs to be a tool to be constant and to be willing to give the best of ourselves. Thanks to self-esteem, we develop emotionally, make wise decisions, appreciate, and accept others as they are. When we learn the value of knowing ourselves, we do it in the same way. We give what we carry inside. How can I love others when I don't love myself? There is no magic wand to change the negative perception that we sometimes have of ourselves or how cruel we can become when we judge ourselves. The only magic of this is to love and accept ourselves far beyond our mistakes, beliefs, values, and reality.

Self-love is the energy you need to live a happy life. Loving yourself means taking care of yourself. Without self-love, one cannot become happy; one cannot build harmonious relationships; self-realization is impossible without painful losses. Someone still believes that loving yourself means being selfish but where is the fine line between self-love and selfishness?

How to distinguish self-love from selfishness

Selfishness is a symptom of a lack of self-love. Selfishness is the consequences of childhood trauma. (Not so selfish and good, as some think).

How an egoist behaves (regardless of gender) does not matter whether it is a man or a woman)

An egoist does what he wants and when he wants, without caring how his actions affect others. Everywhere he puts himself in the first place, he wants everything to be the way he needs, at all costs, regardless of others and at the same time, he does not care about the feelings, inconveniences of others. He blatantly transcends other people's boundaries in pursuit of his goals.

The egoist considers his opinion and position to be the only correct one. An egoist does not know how to be grateful. If he gets something from others, then he takes it for granted. He believes that people are obliged to give him what they want. Or selectively grateful (to those who are beneficial to him). The egoist skillfully manipulates other people's feelings. He puts himself above others, consciously or unconsciously, each time proving to himself that he is worth something.

The egoist is looking for someone else's attention. He needs to be well spoken of, admired, and praised. Otherwise, it is difficult for him to feel himself the center of the universe. If he does something for other people, it is only to please his ego. The egoist acts out of lack (lack of love, lack of attention, etc.), so he needs it more than anyone else. He takes from the outside, consumes. He does not share because he believes that he is not enough. It follows that the egoist does not love himself.

His heart, the source of love, is blocked. And even if he wants to share with someone something (material or not material), he will definitely wait, sometimes even demand a return. He will be offended and indignant.

The egoist does not notice his mistakes. And if something went wrong, then others are to blame. Selfishness is immaturity, trauma, and nothing to do with the manifestation of healthy self-love. For an egoist, thoughts, words, and actions diverge. Such "self-love" always has some hidden nuances. There is no consistency. At home with family, a person with manifestations of selfishness "builds" everyone, manipulates (through fear, through his resentment), keeps the family in constant tension, and at work allows the boss to treat himself disrespectfully, ingratiate himself, and love. (Or not with the boss, but with someone else, a girlfriend or boyfriend)

Egoist, this is a big child who never learned to be an adult. Many joys of life are unknown to him. Selfish behavior can manifest itself in each of us under certain circumstances. And knowing this, you can change it. The relationship to others and the relationship to oneself should not be the opposite!

Self-love before seeking love in others

We all have a friend who is always looking for love, looking everywhere, he just does not want to be alone or alone in this world, and sometimes, we notice how desperate he is.

Beyond judging these types of people, I think we have to be more empathetic, they are probably trying so hard to feel loved or love someone, and that is why they are out there waiting for the right person. To work on self-love, it is important to try to love yourself in all your phases. The most important thing is always the work of emotions. When I realized that working on my emotions was more important than my exterior, I learned to see my value as a human being. If you still don't know how to work inside yourself, I recommend analyzing what makes you feel uncomfortable with yourself. Many times we feel insecure about things that others probably don't even notice. Remember that psychological therapy is part of the basic basket, so don't be afraid to ask a professional for help.

Self-love is in front of the mirror

If you don't believe me, stand in front of the mirror in the morning and say out loud, "I am a valuable person, and I deserve to love myself as much as others."The day you manage to love yourself for what it is, for what it has, for what it fails, and above all, for what it makes you, you will understand that love is not sought in someone else but within you.

In general, human beings live looking for constant approval from our parents, our friends, and especially from our partners, but you know something, the greatest approval you can have is your own, so to work that interior before the exterior.

Do what makes you happy

If you have already worked on your interior and are full and happy, then it is time to work on the exterior, and here comes the part where you will begin to feel full and happy for who you are and what you are building. Everything starts with accepting yourself as you are. Remember that there are things that you can change about yourself and others with which you have to learn to live and work, so there is no option to give up.

The day I decided to change my lifestyle, I became a happier person. I dedicated myself to taking control of my destiny. Do not be afraid of being wrong. People can criticize you, you can fail and fall again and again, but the important thing is that you get up and look for the strength within. Fight for what you want!

References

Amichai-Hamburger, Y. & Vinitzky, G. (2010). Social network use and personality. Computers in Human Behavior, 26, 1289-1295.

Boyd, D. M., & Ellison, N. B. (2007). Social network sites: Definition, history, and scholarship. Journal of Computer-Mediated Communication, 13, 210–230.

Chou, H.-T. G., & Edge, N. (2012). "They are happier and having better lives than I am": The impact of using Facebook on perceptions of others' lives. Cyberpsychology, Behavior, and Social Networking, 15, 117–121.

Clarissa Silva, Social Media's Impact On

Self-Esteem (2020, December) Retrieved from

huffpost.com

Feinstein, B. A., Hershenberg, R., Bhatia, V., Latack, J. A., Meuwly, N., & Davila, J. (2013). Negative social comparison on Facebook and depressive symptoms: Rumination as a mechanism. Psychology of Popular Media Culture, 2, 161–170.

Feinstein, B. A., Hershenberg, R., Bhatia, V., Latack, J. A., Meuwly, N., & Davila, J. (2013).

Negative social comparison on Facebook and depressive symptoms: Rumination as a mechanism. Psychology of Popular Media Culture, 2, 161–170.

Forest, A. L., & Wood, J. V. (2012). When social networking is not working: Individuals with low self-esteem recognize but do not reap the benefits of self-disclosure on Facebook. Psychological Science, 23, 295–302.

Goffman, E. (1959) The Presentation of Self in Everyday Life. Harmondsworth: Penguin.

Heatherton, T. F., & Polivy, J. (1991). Development and validation of a scale for measuring self esteem. Journal of Personality and Social Psychology, 60, 895–910.

Heatherton, T. F., & Polivy, J. (1991). Development and validation of a scale for measuring self- esteem. Journal of Personality and Social Psychology, 60, 895–910.

Heatherton, T. F., & Wyland, C. (2003). Assessing self-esteem. In S. Lopez and R. Snyder, (Eds.), Assessing positive psychology (pp. 219–233). Washington, DC: APA.

Homans, George C. 1961. Social Behavior: Its Elementary Forms. New York: Harcourt, Brace and World, Inc.

Jessica Cho, How Social Media Can Affect Your Self Esteem (2020, December) Retrieved from https://www.healthcorps.org/how-social-media-can-affect-your-self-esteem/

Laurent Francois, Digital Love: How We Fall in Love in the Era of Social Media (2020, December) Retrieved from https://www.socialmediatoday.com/content/digital-love-how-we-fall-love-era-social-media

Mehdizadeh, S. (2010). Self-presentation 2.0: Narcissism and self- esteem on Facebook. Cyberpsychology, Behavior, and Social Networking, 13, 357–364.

Moreno, M., & Kolb, J. (2012). Social networking sites and adolescent health. Pediatric Clinics of North America, 59(3), 601-612.

Morse, S., & Gergen, K. J. (1970). Social comparison, self- consistency, and the concept of self. Journal of Personality and Social Psychology, 16, 148–156.

Pew Research Internet Project 2013. "Frequency of Social Media Use." Washington, DC: Pew Research Center. Retrieved November 2020 (http://www.pewinternet.org/2013/12/30/frequency--of--social--media--use/)

Rae Jacobson, Social Media and Self-Doubt (2020, December) Retrieved from https://childmind.org/article/social-media-and-self-doubt/

Silje Steinsbekk et al (2020). The impact of social media use on appearance self-esteem from childhood to adolescence—A 3-wave community study, Computers in Human Behavior. DOI: 10.1016/j.chb.2020.106528

Tazghini, S. & Siedlecki, K. (2013). A mixed approach to examining Facebook use and its relationship to self-esteem. Computers in Human Behavior, 29, 827-832.

Tosun, L. P. (2012). Motives for Facebook use and expressing the "true self" on the

Internet. Computers in Human Behavior, 28, 1510– 1517.

Valkenburg, P. M., Peter, J., & Schouten, M. A. (2006). Friend networking sites and their relationship to adolescents' well-being and social selfesteem. Cyber Psychology & Behavior, 9, 584 – 590.

Victoria Hoff, Self-Love in the Age of Social Media (2020, December) Retrieved from https://thethirty.whowhatwear.com/self-love-social-media/slide3

Vitak, J., & Ellison, N. (2013). "There's a network out there you might as well tap": Exploring the benefits of and barriers to exchanging informational and support-based resources on Facebook. New Media and Society, 15, 243–259.

Vogel, E., Rose, J. P., Roberts, L. R., & Eckles, K. (2014). Social comparison, social media, and self-esteem. Journal of Educational Policy and Entrepreneurial Research, 2(1), 87-92.

Self-Love vs. Digital Lust

Made in the USA
Columbia, SC
16 March 2021